The Story of Keiko & Niko

Can you find the bone in every picture?

This book is dedicated to all of the amazing owners of bully breed dogs that have ignored the breeds' unwarranted negative reputation and given them the love and respect that they deserve.

Special thanks to: Natalie Rankin - this book wouldn't be a book without you. Len Foley and Rebecca Gauthier - your advice and guidance played a huge role in this project. Melissa Nackovski - your support has been everything. My husband for being the best dog dad Keiko and Niko could ask for. Simi Valley Missing Pets for saving our dogs' lives - without you, we wouldn't know the tremendous joy these dogs have brought to our family. My mom and dad for your ongoing love and support.

Some extra special thanks to my junior editors - Owen, Connor M., Reese, Madison, Andrew, Molly, Ellie, Liam, Fynlie, Kendal, EJ, Bailey, Breena, Bevin, Isabella, Hattie, Declan, Theodore, Sara, Connor C., Kai, Tadashi, Melissa and Jimi.

Our cute bandanas and onesies by The Plus Size Pooch on www.theplussizepooch.com.

Published by Tawny Minami Publishing
ISBN 978-1-7358883-2-3
©2020 Tawny Minami

All rights reserved. No part of this book may be reproduced or transmitted in any form or by any means whatsoever without express written permission from the author, except in the case of brief quotations embodied in critical articles and reviews. Please refer all pertinent questions to the publisher.

Contact or Follow us:
www.keikoandniko.com
Instagram: @keiko.and.niko
Facebook: Keiko.and.Niko

Hi! My name is Keiko. I am a very sweet pitbull. This is the story about me and my brother Niko.

I have five brothers and sisters. We were all saved by some really nice rescue people and then adopted by different families. We were four months old when each of us were adopted.

I was so lucky because I was adopted by the best paw-rents! They gave me everything I needed: yummy food, fun toys, a soft bed with blankies and lots and lots of love.

Even though I was so happy and loved by my new family, I wondered if my brothers and sisters were as lucky with their new families.

Eight months later, my paw-rents saw online that my brother Niko was up for adoption again!

It turns out the first family that adopted Niko was not very nice to him. They decided they could no longer take care of him. The kind rescue people took him back so they could find a loving forever home for Niko.

Can you guess what happened next?

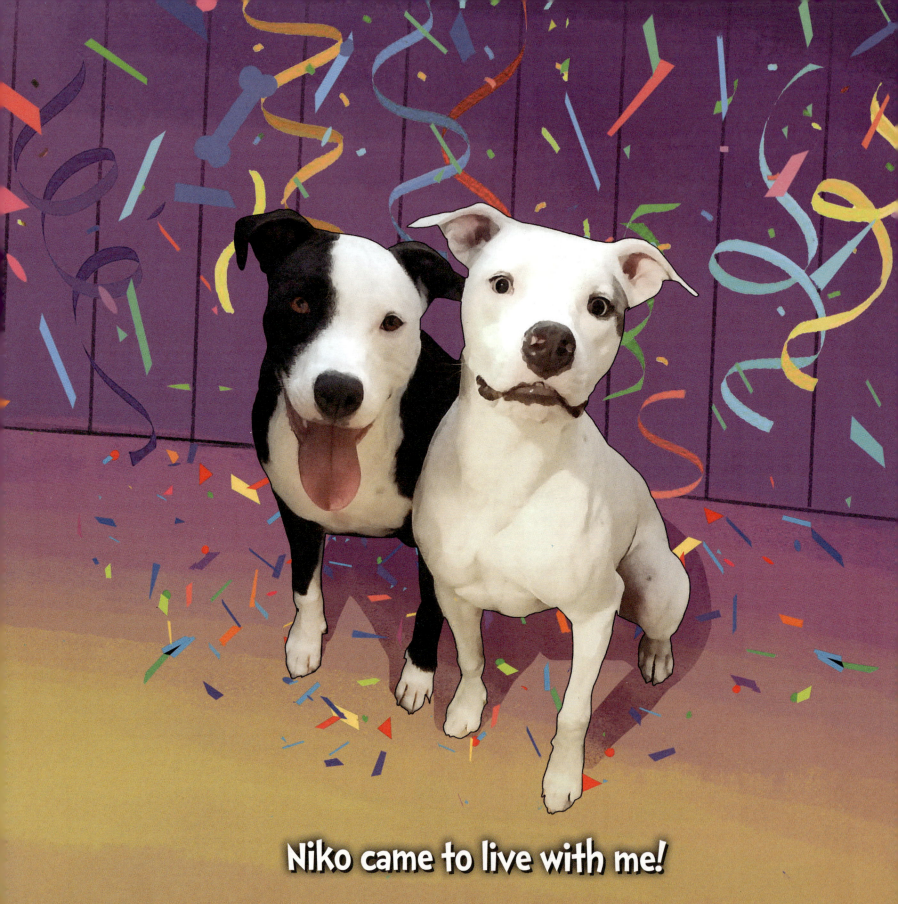
Niko came to live with me!

On Niko's first night with us, I climbed into his crate and we cuddled all night long.

Sometimes Niko needs a little extra love in order to feel safe and I'm happy to give him all the love he needs.

Niko and I are inseparable now. He would rather sleep with me than by himself on his bed, so we nap together on one bed.

When it's time to go to bed for the night, we sleep next to each other covered in our blankies.

We share one dog house because we like to snuggle.

KEIKO & NIKO

Our mommy loves having us dress up and wear bandanas... lots of them!

For special occasions, we get dressed up and even get to wear bowties.

But most of the time we just chill out on the couch together.

We are just SO happy to be together again!

I love having my brother back!

About the Author

Tawny Minami has lived in the beautiful state of California her whole life. She and her husband have been the proud paw-rents of four amazing dogs, two of which have passed away after long, happy lives. They now live in Southern California with their sweet boys, Keiko and Niko.

Their first dog, Onara, is the dog that changed Tawny's mind about pitbulls. When they rescued what they thought was a lab puppy, the vet let them know that she was actually a lab/pitbull mix. Unfortunately, up until this point, Tawny was uneducated about the breed and believed the negative stigma about pitbulls. Onara was the sweetest, most gentle love bug and Tawny's mind was forever changed about this amazing breed.

Changing the reputation of pitbulls and bully breeds is a big passion of Tawny's which is why she wanted to tell the sweet story of Keiko and Niko. She has an Instagram page @keiko.and.niko that is dedicated to showing how amazing these dogs are and that they deserve the same love and respect as any other breed. "If this book or my Instagram page helps to open people's minds and hearts to bully breeds, then I will be happy."